um,
n, but
but   um,
   butum, but
butum,   butum,
, budum, budum,
, budum, dum, dum,
um, dum, tum, tum, tum,
m, tumtum, tumtum, tumtum,
n, tumtum, tumtum budum, tumtum
, tumtum budum, tumtum budum, tum-
dum, tumtum tiddy tum, tumtum tiddy tum,
n tiddy tum, tumtum tiddy tum, tumtum tiddy
tum,   tum, tumtum tiddy tum budum,
m   tumtum tiddy tum budum, tum-
                  tum tiddy tum budum, tumtum
                  tiddy tum budum, tumtum tiddy tum
                  budum, tum, tiddy, but um, tum, tiddy,
                  but um, tum, tiddy, but um, tum, tiddy, but
                  um, tum, tiddy, but um, um, but, but um, but
                  um, but um, but um, but um, but um, butum,
                  butum, butum, butum, butum, budum, budum,
                  budum, budum, budum, dum, dum, dum, dum, dum,
                  tum, tum, tum, tum, tum, tumtum, tumtum, tumtum,
                  tumtum, tumtum, tumtum budum, tumtum budum, tum-
                  tum budum, tumtum budum, tumtum budum, tumtum
                  tiddy tum, tumtum tiddy tum, tumtum tiddy tum, tumtum
                  tiddy tum, tumtum tiddy tum, tumtum tiddy tum budum,
                  tumtum tiddy tum budum, tumtum tiddy tum budum, tum-
                  tum tiddy tum budum, tumtum tiddy tum budum, tum, tiddy,
                  but um, tum, tiddy, but um, tum, tiddy, but um, tum, tiddy, but
                  um, tum, tiddy, but um, um, but, but um, But um, but um, but
                  um, but um, but um, butum, butum, butum, butum, butum,
                  budum, budum, budum, budum, budum, dum, dum, dum, dum,
                  dum, tum, tum, tum, tum, tum, tumtum, tumtum, tumtum, tum-
                  tum, tumtum, tumtum budum, tumtum budum, tumtum
                  budum, tumtum budum, tumtum budum, tumtum tiddy tum,
                  tumtum tiddy tum, tumtum tiddy tum, tumtum tiddy tum, tum-
                  tum tiddy tum, tumtum tiddy tum budum, tumtum tiddy tum
                  budum, tumtum tiddy tum budum, tumtum tiddy tum budum,
                  tumtum tiddy tum budum, tum, tiddy, but um, tum, tiddy, but
                  um, tum, tiddy, but um, tum, tiddy, but um, tum, tiddy, but um,
                  um, but, but um, but um, but um, but um, but um, but um,
                  butum, butum, butum, butum, butum, budum, budum,
                  budum, budum, budum, dum, dum, dum, dum, dum, tum,
                  tum, tum, tum, tum, tumtum, tumtum, tumtum, tumtum,
                  tumtum, tumtum budum, tumtum budum, tumtum
                  budum, tumtum budum, tumtum budum, tumtum
                  tiddy tum, tumtum tiddy tum, tumtum tiddy tum,
                  tumtum tiddy tum, tumtum tiddy tum, tumtum tiddy
                  tum budum, tumtum tiddy tum budum, tumtum
                  tiddy tum budum, tumtum tiddy tum budum,
                  tumtum tiddy tum budum, tum, tiddy, but um,
                  tum, tiddy, but um, tum, tiddy, but um, tum,
                  tiddy, but um, tum, tiddy, but um, um, but,
                  but um, But um, but um, but um, but
                  um, but um, butum, butum, butum,
                  butum, butum, budum, budum,
                  budum, budum, budum, dum,
                  dum, dum, dum, dum, tum,
                  tum, tum, tum, tum, tum-
                  tum, tumtum, tumtum,
                  tumtum, tumtum, tum-
                  tum budum, tumtum
                  budum, tumtum budum,
                  tumtum budum, tumtum
                  budum, tumtum tiddy
                  tum, tumtum tiddy tum,
                  tumtum tiddy tum, tum-
                  tum tiddy tum, tumtum
                  tiddy tum, tumtum tiddy
                  um budum, tumtum tiddy
                  um budum, tumtum tiddy
                  m budum, tumtum tiddy
                  n budum, tumtum tiddy
                  n budum, tum, tiddy, but
                  tum, tiddy, but um, tum,
                  , but um, tum, tiddy, but
                  um, tiddy, but um, um, but,

Jordan Scott | blert

Coach House Books | Toronto

first edition

 Canada Council   Conseil des Arts
for the Arts   du Canada
 ONTARIO ARTS COUNCIL
CONSEIL DES ARTS DE L'ONTARIO
Canadä

Published with the generous assistance of the Canada Council
for the Arts and the Ontario Arts Council. Coach House Books
also acknowledges the support of the Government of Ontario
through the Ontario Book Publishing Tax Credit and the
Government of Canada through the Book Publishing Industry
Development Program.

LIBRARY AND ARCHIVES CANADA
CATALOGUING IN PUBLICATION

Scott, Jordan, 1978-
    Blert / Jordan Scott.

Poems.
ISBN 978-1-55245-199-1

    I. Title.

PS8587.C6254B54 2008   C811'.6   C2008-901490-1

For those who do

It is part of my existence to be the parasite of metaphors, so easily am I carried away by the first simile that comes along. Having been carried away, I have to find my difficult way back, and slowly return, to the fact of my mouth.

Their thick tongues blort, eyes squeeze grief, a crowd
of huge unheard answers jam and rejoice –

What's wrong?

blort   jam   rejoice

Some will not when by themselves.
Some will not when speaking to children or animals.
Some will not when they sing.

What is the utterance?

Phonemes flounder briquette warmth. Tethered to seven molluscs, an osteoblast chomps into the burger of kelp's wreck; an osteoclast nibbles a puffin's scapula in mid-afternoon weight. Each webbed foot tussles, the soft hum of slipper on hardwood floors.

What is the utterance?

Dewlap syllables Mesozoic. The billabong passes as gung-ho through scaffolded throats, blotches lobule curves until Mesozoic ricochets cochlea, at a slow freight. The palate thermoregulates, camouflages, the antelope roll.

What is the utterance?

My mouth drew the swallow's panic. Chew pteryla. The spaces between them chomp apterium; gizzard beat Broca, Broca. Chirped electrode. Sing *fuming*. Sing *furious*. Now, open your mouth and speak. Incisive fossa in labial turbulence, sing *fuming*, sing *furious*. In neuroimaging, filoplumes blitz. Now open your mouth and speak. Sing *frumious*.

What is the utterance?

What a poor crawling thing you are!

Buccal slinks into hoodoo. The dawn clots oort. Bruise syllabic upon upturned halibut, welded to sky curve. We watch, in a book toss, the yap blip, and in careful, clasp to each blurt, clug clug the sherbet angles of vowel's echolalia. Trash lip, lisp smudge: July, mucus, raspberry. Inside, a toothful jujube purls comma. We'll all meet on the tongue. We'll all meet in the tongue. Pickaxe plosive bloat and say: *b is for* by the mouth's slight erosions.

If you must repeat, blowgun bleat. Tip Phyllobates, masticate equation: word order = world ardour.

In frame, then frame, we rumba smooth across laminate as lamprey weave gorgonian pores. Above us, tunnels splatternite muggy. We rappel, frantic drips to harzburgites, spelunk carpal a soda straw to outwash, we – excess, wine must have gestured influx, bent knee, hamates wicket belay, Roosa light plunder esophagus. We blitz horizon, the Petzl Ecrin sheds its carbon, each trona pinnacle dust to tonsil, our phlegm spicules, boil saline paces until strata suffocate and release from tile, until coragyp gyres, the burst of hippus, a corneal Richter, box jellyfish, fleck arrhythmic bambuca.

In chassis, then exoskeleton, we xongo smooth across marble as eel weave coral hole. Above us, burrow splatternite humid. We parry, berserk trickle to harzburgites, spelunk digit a soda straw to brackish, we – excess, wine would have signalled influx, warped patella, hamates wicket crampon, Roosa light ransack esophagus. We assault horizon, the Edelrid Ecrin sheds its monoxide, each tufa spire soot to lymphoid, our mucus spicules, bubble saline tempo until strata suffocate from thermoplastic, until vulture pirouettes, the shiver of hippus, an epithelium Richter, punch chironex, dapple arrhythmic merengue.

At some point you mention circumlocution, but my mouth just isn't working today. You say, 'Looks like a pinnacle karst, oolithic karst, a boulder choke of spitzkarren ahead,' and I trek textured in chomp, rappel lingual, and hiss a plankton paprika into the pitch of long words.

Some whoop and flounder.

Hiccup the sandbag of each letter, ravenous for breath's wind-tunnel billow.

So all fondle the fables that promise.

Dribble of spit trapezes C's geometry. Phlegm scrum knuckles hum; consonant gobstop corpse in clot. I know its textile from the typography of your lips: your scrunch an' munch, your Blistex baboon. How C Pezes snorkel until pfft-pfft belly-flops against H's amoeba rhythm. How, squat in glottal, I bugles a gorilla orchestra, and C cleats and pickaxes up from lungs. And how, in shame, H teeter-totters back into the warm of throat and still larvae A. RA-RA skiddles percussion. Each squawk box blorff xylophones nougat goo. Pancake fold vocal, garble lullaby:

Pukapuka chunder, gut bugs obese buzz: *Chachalaca zizz, chocoholic zest, chinchilla zong, chillastic zouk, chainsaw zing, Chechen zilch, chug zit, chirp zap.*

Nacho flip CH CH in a mouthful goiter. Tongue and canine boing-boing until CH CH knockout chipmunk achoo. Until CH hush crustacean and opera urchin fable:

The chichara has to sing inside the mouth.

A trochanter accordion bellow: bubble-jet into your mouth dome. Moist timbals pus kazoo into jaw marrow. And you will chatterbox, blob the barbs of C with honey and herd glottal stops out the lips. You will learn to use your mouth.

I find one in that field torn in two by the train tracks. Kneel down in the grass, and it leaps at me. Hold it by its middle, raise it to the sun. Legs pedal slow through heat.

I open, shovel bug on tongue. Swing teeth into lip. Cicada for Chiclet. Trident itch. Pluck mucus in harpsichord. Tickle and rondo obese on the palate, blubbers weather into my body: a dry rasp, lick of curved blue. The coxa, hot, jitters syllable, zippers cheek walls: CH, CH, CH hacksaws chichara into glossed walls of teeth.

If you stand in the grass with me. *Wait.* If you graze patella to crust, you will see my mandible rustle a quiet tectonic. *Wait.* You will see the tarsus machete each tentacle-bundled syllable. *Wait.* You will see the panicked pharynx ratchet the tale. *Wait.* You will see the inside: a stuck thorax, a tibia limp and ocelli lantern the fluent C – useless in the narrative.

chomp set

glacial jiggy

if you must have an idea, have a short-term idea:

a Cocoa Puff
a two-step bluff
a fleeting rime

lactic acrobat
pretzel lumbar
licorice ganglia
crackulates scapula
calliope tremor coccyx:

crypt walk
jaw arctic

Interac tracheal
soundtrack:

ice-wedge Nebraskan crevasse

ligament wrench
turret mangrove gambol:
Morocco Morocco
dust mukluk stomp

alveoli necking
crust lithostatic
six-pack copy that
wrench tarsus
limp like that
lichen cramp

fat burlap

fondle felsic
algae cramp
menstruate

moraine kickback
litter scarp

flub hubbub
mug Humboldt
current lub
upwell hummer
bumble axial
tilt jumble
double trouble

tonsil box stucco
dermis a glacial Etch A Sketch
liplock knob

bulimic esker

Weather pincer vellum. Blizzard octave: Spitsbergen Spitsbergen. Tonsils click hummocky, sound of hummingbirds drenched in glacial milk. At this time of year, ice gumshoe chin choreography. Chub flutter at ruckus pace. Chops drudge. Jellies blimp kisser. Barbell tentacles lasso tooth. Goo cuddle glottal. Gel cadence stickum outside the syllable: *and you will quiet, Lycra cinched to a manta ray, lazy, in blue-burn shallows.*

Lagoon waddles in chew. Harmonics vomit the rest.

Jug band collagen grunt gibbon. Gumslurp volcanism, aa as lumberjack ochre clumps mud flap thigh in thick spittoon octane.

Ski-Doo os coxae boomps-a-daisy the calyx whorl in Rupp Dayco drive belt. Spew pollen. Popcorn cumulus glaze Brash Ice:

nankang break stand thaw nunatak

Frigid chitchat couscous goosebumps to fibula. Ugg walk. Unk unk talk. Jukebox cleft Rubik's mucus. Call box jowl Tetris spit. Each bombast cheek pouch thromb amp protozoan. Adjectives drumlin tongue. Beneath the bergs, chatter scallop, a hypothermic gab against baleen's amphitheatre:

Tuktoyaktuk kerplunk
prawn throat.

Imitate: frazil ice. Say clacra, frazil ice, clacracla.
Imitate: muskoxen. Say flafra, muskoxen, flafrafla.

Urchin scattergun larval plume an iris-thick gelatin flops coral's cerebellum. Mesoderm gluts. Urchin bloom. Mucus hue, pink plume, spindles aerobic tentacles to chuck cocoons riddled with Ordovician retinas, haunt yellow as lilac grains. Plankton crumbs hum in current soak, pry buccinators for photophore hunt, or the syllable for gill.

Narwhal back arc spasms pancake ice as alder root sambas soil phonic dipslip mukluk harpoon croon sonar's marrow hip – dipped arctic cream bongs tusk knots.

Echo calving cuckoo, blip chorus:

gales bend citrus as language in June
hyphen tear muscles monsoon

bladderwracked glottal
woofer snorkel
the syllable pinballed

algae Tang

Mandible chatter, a Gatling hopscotch:

herring clatter buccal cove; yokel coconut acoustic

Plankton trek trachea, an ice-packed high-top waltz. Walrus flop tongue, chomp tusk onto ice sizzle. Air sac ebb: eco racket dome slow ice furrow, dorsal rip katabatic overflow, tectonic chattermarks rip-rap frazil ice. Mucus globs gumbotill until syrup sweet lymph between words.

Rehearse in verse. Horn spit. Rest. Speedbag glottal. Rise. Bumblebee yodel. Again.

Consider efficiency, the second bicuspid in manic syllabic
husk. Consider the esophagus, the gather; bushels stalk
esophagus, burn cane in alveoli. Consider the combine,
lip toss, molar churn; given the harvest, worth the rico-
cheting, worth the glitch.

What is the rhythm?

Tendon slurp: Caretta caretta. The sheet like respiratory muscles.

What is the rhythm?

Bramble harmonizes with glottal percussion, drenched plastron
in tadpole gelatin. Each alien orb jengas, a honeycomb grill for
the syllable ascent. Mouth frond, spore sutsuts. In tongue
slumber, each swollen tangos T's stomp Broca, until blackberry
mush. The larynx drools redness as spawn. A boy jabs his molars,
thinks a dew worm folds onto the barb, thinks its curl stings cello
against his own enunciation.

What is the rhythm?

Turtle scaffolds larynx. Globs flipper to palate, flutter jugular
with serum jabber. On each cuspid, the want of sound tumble
muscle as gymnasts; the low whine of their stressed abdominals
dreads the sloth, toward the lips.

What is the rhythm?

All the interim is.

The gaps between the syllables are filled by the frivolous guesses and surmises of birds.

You monsoon across the alphabet, croon turbulence and whisper: *A is for alligator,* against the Mississippi marooned on my gums. Gumbo thrums from lips and you drizzle glossary, soak into *S* like your throat gurgles the wrung-out cotton from a humid Zandunga: *Say S, say sathasha sashatha, say spoon.* I hiss and that is all. *Say S, shass shassha, say …* gymnasts squat bulk quads atop your tongue, S somersaults warm into P and I geyser, hoot, O-O at this alphabetic kinetic. *Say S, say shrathra shrathrashra, say spoon.* Your pucker hunkers in singsong:

When zigzags of zebra finches regurgitate the sky a dumb purple, you must put a spoon in your mouth and clap clams for wet tinkerbells. You will lunge your thorax into spring. Open wide – and pollen, like cotton balls, will faint from your lips onto the pawpaw papaya of next syllable. You will learn the drawl of apricot, roll core in glottal, and drool quiet in the comma. You will sing like the birds.

In that field torn in two by train tracks, I lie down on my back. Pick nose, pick noises, pluck bugs, pump hula hoop, slingshot grasshoppers into throat's long black sleeves. Bloated in wait, my mantra chunk: will not imagine myself as a giant mouth. Will not think that words are enormous. Will not chew gum, or put gobstoppers, lollipops or toffee in my mouth before the finches drown the sky with their hollow bones.

At dusk the sun ughed against horizon and the finches bruised the sky purple. I put the spoon in my mouth. Ziplocked lip to tin. I put the spoon in my mouth, incisor chunks bunt, bunt,

bunt to Pango Pango sky. Wingpit spoons the hyoid frantic. Ebb ebb clanks palate in hallux drag. The birds were in my mouth. Feathered clumps sop up mucus, peck plaque for pomegranate, doo-wop glottal stop, talon and lore toward lung's perch.

I take the spoon out of my mouth. Open wide. Wait for trill. Open wide. Will not mumble, will not slur, will not dread the word, will not chew gum, or put gobstoppers, lollipops or toffee in my mouth before each vocal tilt flirts cuckoo. If you brace a megaphone to my throat, you will hear a tiddlywink bleat, a lark rustle in the ripe corn, and my esophagus blunderbuss – exhaust in your glossary.

Genus: zebra finch (Taeniopygia guttata)

Call: rapid nasal stops: bunt, bunt, bunt // 7 percent of zebra finches stammer with intermittent yak yak (like syllables).

Behaviour: 'They learned to mumble – not to speak – and it was only after paying attention to the increasing noise of the century, and after they got whitened by the foam of its crest, that they acquired a language.' – *Australian Finches in Bush and Aviary*

Algae crumples under radar's tiddlywink bleat. Ghetto blaster perches clavicle, brackish treble culls Tetrax tetrax: oom oom makak oom oom makak … gyred pogo style to hibachi picnic. Mandible kabobs cram operculum. The mollusc husked hotly:

Macaque fandangos. Humpbacked gudunkadunk bump-and-grind trunk in Tumtum tree. Each thumb bushwhacks as cranked-up Muzak bric-a-bracs.

Pica pica in rumpus banter, a humongous flock, an Amazonian jamboree! Toucan raptorial jam scaffolds kapok bark. Vocal irk nunchuks ZsaZsa – phlegm as linen or mink, slung each Caracara dihedral. Bumblebees zombie cantaloupe, buzz Guadeloupe until dark:

Brontosaurus lambada boom box, crunk bumps: knick-knack paddy whack tonsil clamcrack.

chomp set

blubber tongue

if you must have an idea, have a short-term idea:

a Cocoa Puff
a two-step bluff
a fleeting rime

Broca's
camel clutch
grapple thalamus flux
box tonsils fresh black box
tongue scatter suckle polygon
syllable collar pop
mullet split end
leg lock glottal
lip off:

fresh nugs
mouse milking
NASCAR

wrist flex
snorkel mosh
dental furrow
Jell-O shot
ease Pantene

Coca-Cola tonic krill
gill baleen
dream wrenched
Kleenex smack
Baltic Pyrex
megahertz humpback
kickback: flex
nukes flub
blubber sexy
plankton number

Foreman rill
grill lisp
dental Whopper

Worcestershire

scaffold larynx
magma seethe
tarp gruff volcanic
ply canine

cusp
munch
crunch
rump

gales lurk
berserk cortex
honeyed botox
globs boom of clavicles
cornsilk lips blitz as
Molotov blisters
Tupperware slur

celeb Tex-Mex
thunder thigh

aerobic gulag
squeeze bottle
Gucci groin

bent tendon
each papyrus
fold cackles
buzz beatbox:
Kyzyl Kum Kyzyl Kum
shizzle cadence
cavum kinetic

Hunch, it is the misdeed of language.

What is the syllable?

Ekstrom hertzed: an orchestra of tendons or bees stretch in a cool piterak. Chandelier hive in frenulum and drawl, the moon grapples with a stubborn tide.

What is the syllable?

Skookumchuck narrows, puckers waka waka against the rush of river. A haboob burst in your pharynx, technoed badunkadunk in zygomaticus major. The cochlear yawn centipedes tattletale in buckthorn orange. Each maxilliped bongos, fresh cornflakes suplex atop enamel.

What is the syllable?

Fog to cleft a passing tango, rank with mashed mango, lobs chunk to crunk the courtyard, lungs to glide the rung-out shards, slang and Lougheed. Cleft and fog trip tango reek with split citrus, spill darkens sod, lungs thrash, slang stacks. Fog to cleft, the tango rank. Each clavicle tides Courvoisier. Lean scythe, fog scatters.

What is the syllable?

You would be for hours beside a wounded walrus, conscious of it, a bone in an x-ray, and for milliseconds in the midst of a tragic wallow.

What is the syllable?

I am sorry to keep you in wait.

*At some moment in early life, when the ink of I anchors in
vocal, there must be a question, a question so powerful
that it is forgotten, because all that is remembered is the
circumstance. The roll-call choral mouths: 'I am present.'
Your turn. The arm raise. The impossibility of speaking
your own lines.*

Not articulated to any other bone, the hyoid bone lounges in the
human neck. Suspended from the tips of styloid ligaments, only
two plump bursas interrupt this hammocked marrow. In early
life, the lateral borders are connected to the voice box by pretend
membrane; after middle life, usually by bony union. The hyoid
bone allows a wider range of tongue and laryngeal movements,
enabling the speaker the ability to tortoise each morpheme up
from the trachea, across the tongue and, eventually, onto lips'
diameter. Some muscles of the root of the tongue are attached to
it, as well as some laryngeal muscles. It is not attached to any
other bone, which it makes it something of a curiosity among
bones.

Hyoid derives its name from the Greek word hyoeides, meaning
shaped like the letter upsilon or U. This hammock, or horseshoe-
shaped bone, has the ability to balm or tranquilize riotous
plosives and/or consonants. Many people who suffer from
broken or corrupted speech have described the hyoid bone as a
cartilage bunker, assaying ambush from the dictionary and
preventing the blitzkrieg of relapse. For most people, however,
the hyoid bone simply allows for eloquence in oration and
success in conversation.

If you wish to become an eloquent speaker, you should bury the
hyoid bone of a lamb in the wall of your house. Lip-lock gyproc

with putty-s'mored lips, put bone in flamingo insulate, a tropic or epiglottic siege. Once installation is complete, the fevered and always consistent Gatling bleat of the lamb will begin to pulp ripe locution into every corner of your abode.

How the kitchen muzzles clang-clang enamel for floured prose beaten and rolled into sense, and how the steam of hot taps saunas the knotted tendons of difficult phrases. How the bathroom fills the tub to tenderize its own plosive, and how the mirror heaves chested silica at such a pace as to dissect words into warm breath, a chronic cloak of your bobbled mouth. How the dining room serves only gelatinous morsels like milkshakes, honey and yogurt, all eager to wheelbarrow glistening mounds of fluency onto your chipped molars, lube and slip and slide like fat suburban men in July into the fertilized throb of your manicured gullet. How, in the bedroom, the adrianople lips of your lover will loaf on marshmallow pillows, opera the vagaries of the day in a flawless Crayola plume. How the curtains wheeze your lungs in unison, a linen waltz of afternoon snooze. How the basement will pickle delicious vocabularies for you to munch on in winter, glossaries of plankton swarming through stringed instruments, crazed glacial pangs for the soft epidermis tundra, and how the basement will store your retainer, night guard and braces, adjacent to the treadmill and elliptical machine, and how the basement will also store your treble-belt tongue and your cobwebbed mandible, for which you have no use anymore.

But, you might ask, how will I speak in these rooms? I answer that you will speak the curve of hyoid, cradle-rock syllable until rockabye acrobatics, and the ache for speech before dream. But know that this speech must be neutral, as undynamic as possible. Speak of bloated whales in turquoise coves, of geodesic domes covered in snow, of trout bellows in warm shallows. But you will not speak of tectonics, of limps, fumbles or dropping utensils; you will not speak of crowded similes or dry mouths. You will not speak of volcanics, of sprints or fevers, you will not speak of tongue tides or oscillographs. As soon as your speech turns to these kinds of activities, or activity of any kind, you will find your body resumes its tension, and when we are tense we cannot progress, and progress is the law of life.

Twa, twaddle, Tweedledee, twas, twayblade, Tweedlededum, twat, tweezers, twinkle-toed, twig, twelve gauge, twin-engined, Twix, twizzle … zizz, zag, Zohar, zone, Zola, zoo, zonked, zoot suit, two

oo, o-o, oolong, oof, ooh, oodles, oom, oort, oozy … oops-a-daisy … een, eerie, eelworm, eek, eejit, eelgrass, eel, eelpout, eensy … chee, chee-chee, cheekbone, cheek, cheerful, cheeky … ye, yearly, yeasty, cheese

sea cow, sea lily, seamy seamstress, sea lion, sea lettuce, sea potato, sea moth, sea holly, sea gooseberry, sea dog, sea nettle, sea elephant, sea bee … beer, beetle, the bee's knees, beef … ff, FBI, ff, FBA, FB … bur, beef bur, Burberry, burb, burgers

SSB, SSC, SSE, SSP, SSR, SST, SSW … WWF … fury, furuncle, fur seal … lee, leer, leek, leech … Chabrol, cha-cha … faff, French bean, French Congo, French bread, French cricket, French curve, French dressing, French

hiccup, hibachi, hickey, hide and seek, hi-fi … Fri, friendly fire, Freedom Fire, fries

SS, SSAFA … A, a, aargh, aardwolf, Ann Landers, Anna Banana, and

D, d, DA … A535, AAA, a

A, Aalborg, aardvark … kaka-beak, kaka-pants, kaka … AK, Akbar, akimbo … Co. c/o cocoa cabana, cockspur, cockeye bob, coconut palm, cock-up, cocksucker, cock and bull, cock block, cockatoo, cock-of-the-walk, cockpit, cochlea, cock-a-leekie, cock-eyed, Coca-Co, O … oak, oaktag, oakum, OAPEC … KKK, Kokanee, Koko, Kit Kat, Coke.

If therapy is a must, wad cakehole Blister Rust. Laminate brank, ingurgitate gospel: word languor = world rancour.

Mouth implies room; room mimics mouth.

In jugular then jujitsu, we ta-ta bazooka-woven nouns. Our femur arrhythmia Slinky's Hubba Bubba onto forcep grip; Blast Off OshKoshB'Gosh in a choir of bing bang bong utensils on linoleum floors. In the room, stucco gills staccato. In the room, typo baboons on jowl. Our chinfest lustres muscovite, clangs jaundice tint to voice: *sing uu-uus, sing tuhuhtuhuh.* Each troglobite grovels lung; each trilobite whispers fossil. We upchuck gush geoduck, until the want of teeth embezzles barbell Oreo in gingivae bake. Until twixt fricative, Snicker clicks; until Heimlich word ore shucks each muscle kerfuffle in dactyl hubble bubble as cactus pricks against quiet parts. It's what wills and will not, tongue uppercut palate Pop Rocks, our mime siphons out the gas.

In aorta then aikido, we tsk-tsk missle-molted clitics. Our hip arrthythmia Slinky's ooh-la-la onto tweezer cinch; Kablooey Lululemon in a belt-out pa-rum-pum-pum-pum of forks 'n' spoons on cobblestone floors. In the crash pad, stucco lungs staccato. In the crib, mistake numbnuts on muzzle. Our clambake glitters igneous, roars tangerine hue to voice: *sing nit-nit, sing kong'-tak-lak-lak.* Each Ozark crawfish apple-polishes bronchial; each anthropod insinuates eolith. We urp pa'ua until the want of dentin embezzles dumbbell Oreo in gum BBQ. Until Caramilk sibilant, Snicker eject; until Heimlich word ore shucks each tissue ballyhoo in spondee hubbly bubbly as burr low-blows your mute meat. It's that and that's that, radix lucky punch Fizz Wizz, our ventriloquy trawls out the crude.

Gate and glottal mount palate, drool the mollusc-husked haptic, glob clavicles chiffon. Its bruised mantle clatters the scarab musk, welts with, rill with, echoic aortas shunt long cyan divots diaphragms.

The pavilion is in the Coquitlam. The grass paces the wet of each day. The photographs of the pavilion, mouth aperture: one boy in the room, his gutturals click warm. The larynx is roomy. The flash cards, megamouth:

marbles mandible
slow tonic
phlegm Pango Pango
green's apples
tumble sea
mulch bumble
marble chunks
enamel smacks
tongue babble

Xerox bruise
onyx hues

Of my mouth and me. Of other people's fluent mouths and me. Of fluency and me. Of me and my mouth. Of me and other people's fluent mouths. Of me and fluency. My mouth and me. Fluent words and me. Other people's fluent mouths and me. Me and my mouth. Me and fluent. Me and other people's fluent mouths.

Umbra marbles drench the ravine slot, divot light, a barreled birch grasps citrus palm as pumice, as coastal groove hulls plunge pool, the cervical troll, pawpaw bract.

It is the onyx grove again, of being a boy prodding his esophagus, marble in its raw state. Mason dorms scent lust. Green-cased dentils. Dormer curves each boxwood lapis, joists pencil tendon, girth with whisper and lisp.

Scribble Kellogg
carpal velvet
to cupboards
metric lichen
Cortical
idyll wharf
tong oyster
mantle mimic
tandem welt

Jaw flex slate; tip crabs, techno as a Tourette tide spaz. A labyrinth, a game. Calcites glut. Cheliped sounds lattice. A single storey of an L shape with one leg ending in a large glass conservatory. Antennas prod the purple porphyry, licking the brickwork in a scuttling fever. Teem telson's glide in tide's fabric burr. Parade pediment with each cartilage dip, the aorta massage, a small podium, the mauve cushion saddling testes. Pillars to the downslope facade.

Scapulas rippled
struts basin

Clashing Pink in full reams of Kleenex. The forearm drenches into kiln craters. The design method faces collapse, inside seams of ulna, the tear stain, or dragged chair leg stilted pine from palm braids. On top, limestone talus scarp, matched breccia laid on coloured paper – sea green, grey, bronze, gold – globed lichen in mannequin form. Apples on a plate. Crow in spokes. Tibia-torqued lattice. The fabric marathoned to weak magnets, spot-welded to hamate bones soaked Gatorade bow electrode. Each turn had patience, a wire chair, grid, lust for the gasp before stationary.

Patella jitterbugged until honeycomb scab to epidermis. Pump mix, the warthog frantic in humid Exo-Terra, its tusk wobbled trailerload moan: boom back lat lat back boom. Visqueen strapped oris, curbs alveoli's verb pack air slack. Granite scab and Slurpee drips mandible, rebars words in optical lobe. The stickleback writhe toothpick waltz on synapse pulse, ventriloquist trill:

geyser grunt
torso binge and purge
Chiquita thick as bog
hoarfrost batter

big gulp

The torso grind against tundra's soft cotton. Cairn as carpal, as brown placemats. Pores of upturned bicuspids kneel between prongs, twist mug imprint, lid off scar. A door onto an elegant hall or a divot of rusting prams. Drill bicuspid as wasp grinds attic pane; halogen fondles curtains, mix watts with pensioner's tea. Chronochromie apraxia tuba, brute carpal drag: percussion tam tam blubber, palate tom tom butte, portico tum tum buccal, plenum tom tom bronchus. Slowly does it every time.

chomp set

ave

if you must have an idea, have a short-term idea:

a Cocoa Puff
a two-step bluff
a fleeting rime

In lacuna, hallelujah. In lagoon, Ojibwa tuba.

Artery ooze wasabi hue, echo hooey: Pashtoon Pashtoon.

Ode awe hush-hush oboe hiccup, ave Velveeta on first-whirl beluga.

Minnow fandango ossify estuary, woo uh-oh in Wang Chung haze.

This hoopla, now hacienda.

This vivisection, now vendetta.

Muffle newfangled vow:

betrothe epigraph halcyon in cyclone.

When asthma, octave amphibian circadian.

When asphyxia, sumo azure Oahu.

You owe caesura mai tais, owe ow lobotomy.

Ohm hemoglobin ouzo; willow vowel orzo.

Exxon harangue; x-ray ave.

Orangutan hover

each chichi hooray.

Your hem-haw exhume Amazon's octane aria:

armadillo harmonica logorrhea

iguana ennui hillbilly.

Now, zygote guava, each verbivore salacious.

Now, appendix escapade, your aha tsunami

trachea origami

Houdini in open wide:

when lingo, autopsy

when bingo, on ice.

Our aria yawn eczema, wrinkle equinox barramundi.

Oyster amaretto Oceania, bamboozle euphonic volcano:

in scuba, didgeridoo

in hula, brouhaha.

Soon, hyena yada yada bayou.

Soon, mahi-mahi grapheme slough.

Each aorta cacophany immune.

Oblige Zippo shush.

Mayonnaise salvo vertebrae malaise.

Ovum genuflect gobsmacked phrase:

hymn phylum inhale, hymnal asylum exhale.

What is in the stomach carries what is in the head.

You lambada glyph; cockatiel into calligraphy like your mouth-wash swills hurricane. Puke gauze sphagnum and purr: *outbreaks will diminish* against the chincherinchee festooned on bronchial, you go on go on, urge backwash cha-cha-cha, homily into boomshackalacka like fungi canoodle sequoia: *say nosh cricket merengue, your turn, say gnash locust meringue.* I blip blip, hijack sasquatch fib and grovel into jungle camo, while you nerf viscera, tryst anemone in the thick of ABCs. Your faucet blotto's parole:

Eat your grasshoppers – bonbon bilobate, cert cercus. Your long crus of incus chillax maxilla, buoyant in vignette. You will take care to open your mouth, crepitate shoo shoo to Band-Aid dollop. Mop up atrium of Listerine tornado slow to Lego toot-sweet. Pig out abdomen in arthropod oodles, sigh hemocyanin, and talkative broods will glue each cheek-wall cocoon. You will learn to eat your grasshoppers.

Find one in that field torn in two by train tracks. Hold it by its middle, raise it to the sun. Antennae prod magenta in turbulence, theremin glissando whoopsie: must yeehaw. Must ram lungs. Must yum-yum. Must silver-tongued.

Kneel down in grass. Flop stomach to boreal. Vertex lick, the pluck mandolin. *Eat your grasshoppers.* Bulldoze invertebrate, gnaw sulcus till ochre splatter. *Eat your grasshoppers.* Snorkel spurious vein till gargle lava. *Eat your grasshoppers,* and hoover full atop the slaughter.

If you periscope my throat, you will see: cricket cremate stridulate, parlance kookaburra eureka, adjectives periwinkle tarantella, and my mouth, full blorff, give up.

'Everything depends upon the way in which language is thought.' – Gilles Deleuze

'Thought is made in the mouth.' – Tristan Tzara

At its base level, *blert* is a text written to be as difficult as possible for me to read. Poetically, the tempo of *blert* (like the pace of my mouth) is of suspension and falter, clinical and personal. Written as a spelunk into the mouth of a stutterer, *blert* is a trek across labial regions, a navigation of tracheal rills, and a full bore squirm inside the mouth's wear and tear.

When I was a boy my father would let me play hooky on 'bad speech days' and take me fishing. On one particular day, while watching the tide undulate against the shore, my father offered a precise ecological equivalent to what had been going on in my mouth: 'You see how that water moves, son? That's how you speak.' Since then I have always imagined my mouth suctioned to all that mimics its movements. I construct thick glossaries of tongue protrusions and rogue waves, enamel grinding and plate tectonics, chin spasms and plankton swarms. I stock up hefty vocabularies to balm the lexical timber that piles in the cortex as a result of muscular difficulties and evade the brash mouth stumble (like all those *who do*) by honing a detailed vocal portfolio of tics and tricks: hem, haw, ditty, hum, *but um*, hum, *like*, croon, trill, avoid, forget, pretend, duet, *hum, ho hum*, sing, whisper, eat, tune, chew, hum, yell, quiet, choir.

Whether aerobic in these tics or exhausted by the habit, a stutterer's interaction with language is remarkably different from that of persons who don't stutter. Socially, the stutterer is deviant, a facial acrobat whooping in the throes of 'Good morning' or 'One cheeseburger please.' Stutterers dread words: they are obsessed and possessed by their painful shapes and technoed beats.

Consonants, gutturals and plosives zombie throughout their dreams. Perversely, they prepare in advance of every conversation. They are permanently drenched – anticipatory – suspended between the thought and its utterance. While all individuals are dysfluent to some extent, what differentiates stutterers from non-stutterers is the frequency and severity of their disfluency and, most importantly, that those hiccups regarded as 'stutters' are accompanied by an acute awareness of a loss of control.

The stutter here appears on its own terms, rejecting the metaphoric, thematic, graphic (a-a-a-a) or representational aspects of this language disturbance. The text is written as if my own gibbering mouth chomped upon the language system, then regurgitated the cud of difference. My symptoms are the agents of composition. Each furious millisecond of personal struggle colliding with language as a rolling gait of words hidden within words, of syllables in cleavage and breach, all erupting as palpable lava on the palate. The burn and crush in your *own* mouth is dysfluency – animating the bobble of your tongue's slight erosions, of glossary grapple and your now-constant ache for smooth. *blert* is written as a threat to coherence, as a child's thick desire to revamp the alphabet, as an inchoate moan edging toward song.

This book would not have been made without the tireless mentoring and rare friendship of Christian Bök, Steven Collis and Nicole Markotić.

For my family, Curtis, Roy and Wiesia. Nothing happens without them. In memory of Audrey Scott, who let me curl up more times that I can remember, and to Debbie Scott for letting me talk without interrupting.

Summer Kalbfleisch for giving her ears to my lines and happiness to my life.

Kevin Connolly for keeping still while I leaned. Alana Wilcox, for totally losing the bet and always believing in the book.

Vancouver: Andrea Actis for mix tapes. Donato Mancini and Guinevere Pencarrick for teeth, hair, crabs and brilliant response. Jason Christie for balls. Jeff Derksen, Nostrovia! Rob Budde for airplane tickets. Rolf Mauer and the staff at New Star Books. Reg Johanson for Toronto walks. Sharon Thesen for Kelowna orchards. The Coq crew. Wayde Compton for conversation.

Calgary: Aaron Giovannone for Sienna walks and Calgary stumbles. Cara Hedley for calls from Winnipeg to Rhodes. Chris Ewart for glorious man sleeps. Derek Beaulieu for that first invitation to dinner when I arrived in Calgary. Weyman Chan for how to ... Nathalie Zina Walschots for pie and workshops. Sandy Lam for extra blankets. All my friends in Calgary who gave me so much laughter and love while writing this book.

Toronto: Adam Seelig for the Golden Noodle. Artist Bloc. Aaron Tucker for edits and night moves. Mark Truscott for reading *blert* when it was just a few pages. Dennis Lee for his words. Margaret Christakos for constant support and courage. Angela Rawlings for emails in Rome and so much care with my words. Conor Green for the spare room. The staff at Coach House Books, Christina, Stan and especially Evan Munday. Thanks also to all my new friends in the Big Smoke, especially Jenny Sampirisi, Bill Kennedy and Jay MillAr.

Scatter: Anuj Parikh for Petra wanders. Alex Porco for *furmious*. Craig Dworkin for response and awe. Jena Sher for a stunning cover. Jessica Grant for emails after the radio. Kevin Killian for kind words. To the staff at the International Writers and Translators Centre of Rhodes, Greece, for warmth and song. I am also grateful to the Canada Council for the time to write.

'Preface on Avoidance' contains lines adapted from *The Street of Crocodiles* and *Sanatorium Under the Sign of the Hourglass* by Bruno Schulz. Page 9 contains lines from 'Faith Healing' by Philip Larkin, a fellow stutterer. The first fable was written in collaboration with Cara Hedley, and the second fable with Andrea Actis. 'What is the syllable?' contains lines adapted from *The Wild Body* by Wyndham Lewis. The epigraph to the third fable contains lines from 'To the Speech Clinic' by Neil Schmitz. The epigraph to 'Marble Bubble Bobble' is from 'The Stutter of Form' by Craig Dworkin; this essay, which engages with *blert* at length, can be found in *Modalities of the Audible*, edited by Marjorie Perloff and Craig Dworkin (forthcoming from University of Chicago Press). The author's note epigraphs are from *a thousand plateaus: capitalism and schizophrenia* and Tristan Tzara's 'The Dada Manifesto on Feeble Love and Bitter Love.' I also heartily thank and acknowledge *Stutter* by Marc Shell, 'He Stuttered' by Gilles Deleuze and all the work of Christof Migone, in particular *Sonic Somatic: Performances of the Unsound Body*.

I would like to thank the editors of the following publications: Ryan Fitzpatrick's MODL Press, housepress, *filling Station*, *Eleven Eleven*, *nypoesi*, *Drunken Boat* and *Shift and Switch: New Canadian Poetry* for publishing excerpts of *blert*.

Originally from Coquitlam, British Columbia, Jordan Scott now wanders between the Pacific and the Shield. Jordan's first book of poetry, *Silt* (New Star Books), was nominated for the Dorothy Livesay Poetry Prize. In the fall of 2006, Jordan worked on the final sections of *blert* while acting as a writer in residence at the International Writers' and Translators' Centre in Rhodes, Greece. Jordan spends the spring and summer slinging canoes at Pitt Lake, the largest freshwater tidal lake in North America.

Typeset in Minion and Gotham
Printed and bound at the Coach House on bpNichol Lane, 2008

Edited for the press by Kevin Connolly
Designed by Alana Wilcox
Cover art and design by Jena Sher

Coach House Books
401 Huron Street on bpNichol Lane
Toronto, Ontario M5S 2G5

416 979 2217
800 367 6360

mail@chbooks.com
www.chbooks.com

```
                                                        t
                                                      but
                                                but  un
                                            um,    but
                                          butum,  butun
                                  um,    butum,   t
                              budum,   budum,   b
                          budum, budum, dum, dun
                      dum, dum, tum, tum, tum, tun
                  tumtum,  tumtum,  tumtum,  tu
              tumtum, tumtum budum, tumtum b
          budum, tumtum tiddy tum, tumtum tiddy tun
      tum tiddy tum, tumtum tiddy tum,        tum,
        tumtum tiddy tum, tumtum tiddy          t u r
      tum budum, tumtum tiddy tum                 t
    budum, tumtum tiddy tum budum,
  tumtum tiddy tum budum, tumtum tiddy
tum budum, tum, tiddy, but um, tum, tiddy,
but um, tum, tiddy, but um, tum, tiddy, but um,
  tum, tiddy, but um, um, but, but um, but um, but
  um, but um, but um, but um, butum, butum,
  butum, butum, butum, budum, budum, budum,
budum, budum, dum, dum, dum, dum, dum, tum, tum,
tum, tum, tum, tumtum, tumtum, tumtum, tumtum,
tumtum, tumtum budum, tumtum budum, tumtum
budum, tumtum budum, tumtum budum, tumtum tiddy
tum, tumtum tiddy tum, tumtum tiddy tum, tumtum tiddy
tum, tumtum tiddy tum, tumtum tiddy tum budum, tumtum
tiddy tum budum, tumtum tiddy tum budum, tumtum tiddy
tum budum, tumtum tiddy tum budum, tum, tiddy, but um,
tum, tiddy, but um, tum, tiddy, but um, tum, tiddy, but um, tum,
tiddy, but um, um, but, but um, But um, but um, but um, but
um, but um, butum, butum, butum, butum, butum, budum,
budum, budum, budum, budum, dum, dum, dum, dum, dum,
tum, tum, tum, tum, tum, tumtum, tumtum, tumtum, tumtum,
tumtum, tumtum budum, tumtum budum, tumtum budum,
tumtum budum, tumtum budum, tumtum tiddy tum, tumtum
tiddy tum, tumtum tiddy tum, tumtum tiddy tum, tumtum
tiddy tum, tumtum tiddy tum budum, tumtum tiddy tum
budum, tumtum tiddy tum budum, tumtum tiddy tum
budum, tumtum tiddy tum budum, tum, tiddy, but um, tum,
tiddy, but um, tum, tiddy, but um, tum, tiddy, but um, tum,
tiddy, but um, um, but, but um, but um, but um, but um, but
um, but um, butum, butum, butum, butum, butum, budum,
budum, budum, budum, budum, dum, dum, dum, dum,
dum, tum, tum, tum, tum, tum, tumtum, tumtum, tumtum,
tumtum, tumtum, tumtum budum, tumtum budum, tum-
tum budum, tumtum budum, tumtum budum, tumtum
tiddy tum, tumtum tiddy tum, tumtum tiddy tum, tum-
tum tiddy tum, tumtum tiddy tum, tumtum tiddy tum
budum, tumtum tiddy tum budum, tumtum tiddy
tum budum, tumtum tiddy tum budum, tumtum
tiddy tum budum, tum, tiddy, but um, tum,
tiddy, but um, tum, tiddy, but um, tum,
tiddy, but um, tum, tiddy, but um, um,
but, but um, But um, but um, but um,
but um, but um, butum, butum,
butum, butum, butum, budum,
budum,   budum,   budum,
budum, dum, dum, dum,
dum, dum, tum, tum, tum,
tum, tum, tumtum, tum-
tum, tumtum, tumtum,
tumtum, tumtum budum,
tumtum budum, tumtum
budum, tumtum budum,
tumtum budum, tumtum
tiddy tum, tumtum tiddy
tum, tumtum tiddy tum,
tumtum tiddy tum, tum-
tum tiddy tum, tumtum
tiddy tum budum, tumtum
tiddy tum budum, tumtum
tiddy tum budum, tumtum
tiddy tum budum, tumt
tiddy tum budum, tum, ti
but um, tum, tiddy, but um,
tiddy, but um, tum, tiddy, bu
tum, tiddy, but um, um, but u
```